You Will Live Forever

You Will Live Forever

Ernest Holmes

CONTENTS

FOREWORD

It is hoped that this book will give the reader many moments of inspiration and comfort.

Part One is Ernest Holmes' great message on immortality.

The four following parts are based on Psalms, Proverbs, Isaiah, and the words of Jesus from which he has selected the most powerful affirmative statements and passages of great beauty.

The simplicity and force of the Bible readings arranged in this manner provide a spiritual insight which makes them an unusual source of help.

The Bible readings are from the King James Version.

You Will Live Forever

"Whither shall I go from thy Spirit? or whither shall I flee from thy presence? If I ascend up into heaven, thou art there. . . . If I take the wings of the morning, and dwell in the uttermost parts of the sea; even there shall thy hand lead me. If I say, Surely the darkness shall cover me; even the night shall be light about me. Yea, though I walk through the valley of the shadow of death, I will fear no evil: for thou art with me. . . .

"Our soul is escaped as a bird out of the snare of the fowlers: the snare is broken, and we are escaped. . . . and there shall be no more death . . . for the former things are passed away. . . . by man came death, by man came also the resurrection of the dead. For as in Adam all die, even so in Christ shall all be made alive. . . . The last enemy that shall be destroyed is death.

"But some man will say, How are the dead raised up? and with what body do they come? . . . There are also celestial bodies, and bodies terrestrial. . . . So also is the resurrection of the dead . . . it is sown in weakness; it is raised in power: it is sown a natural body; it is raised a spiritual body. There is a natural body, and there is a spiritual body.

"And so it is written . . . The first man is of the earth, earthy: the second man is the Lord from heaven. . . . And as we have borne the image of the earthy, we shall also bear the image of the heavenly."

These words were written nearly two thousand years ago, perhaps on an occasion when a beloved member of someone's family or a dear friend had passed from this world, leaving behind only the memory of a life well lived and well loved.

Then, as now, self-preservation was the first law of life. And someone asked: Is it really true that man has a soul, and if so, is he immortal, and under what circumstances?, Is there really a spiritual body, and do we all, after leaving this body, go on to another one?

For thousands of years before this question was asked, there had been a teaching that this physical body is but an instrument for the spirit and when, by reason of any fact, it is no longer a fit instrument, then the spirit quietly severs itself from the body.

As *The Song Celestial* so beautifully said:

> Never the spirit was born;
> The spirit shall cease to be never;
> Never was time it was not;

End and Beginning are Dreams!

Birthless and deathless and changeless
Remaineth the spirit forever;
Death hath not touched it at all,
Dead though the house of it seems!

Nay, but as one who layeth
His worn-out robes away,
And, taking new ones, sayeth,
"These will I wear today!"

So putteth by the spirit
Lightly its garb of flesh,
And passeth to inherit
A residence afresh.

For thousands of years there had been a teaching that this physical universe is but a counterpart of a spiritual one; that the invisible things of God, as the Bible states, are made manifest or known by the visible; that this physical world is but a symbol or a token of an invisible spiritual universe in which even now we live; and that there is a counterpart or a parallel between the two worlds.

And so when someone asked: How is it that the dead are raised up, and with what body? The question was answered by: "There are also celestial bodies, and bodies terrestrial. . . . There is a natural body, and there is a spiritual body," and all men will some day inherit this spiritual body.

When the disciples of Jesus asked him: What is God's relationship to the dead? he answered, as we should expect, by saying: "God is not a God of the dead, but of the living: for all live unto him." This is not only an inspirational answer by a spiritual genius, it is a logical answer by a great thinker, for God is life and life cannot produce death. Science knows of no energy that can destroy itself.

There are no dead people in my Father's house. Jesus really said: "In my Father's house are many mansions: if it were not so, I would have told you. I go to prepare a place for you. . . . that where I am, there ye may be also. . . . for it is your Father's good pleasure to give you the kingdom."

This teaching is the basic principle of the great and profound philosophy of the Christian faith: that every man is an immortal soul on the pathway of an eternal evolution, destined to be ever more and never less himself, on and on and on.

There are "many mansions," many planes of self-expression. We pass from one to the other; as we die to one, we become resurrected to the other. For every death there is a resurrection, and for every resurrection there must be a death. Not a death of the soul, but a death of the particular form or body we now use. But we are all human beings and we do long for "the touch of a vanished hand, and the sound of a voice that is still."

Yes, we are all human. We miss our friends, we miss their presence, because love and friendship are the greatest things in the world. Love is the lodestone of life, it is the greatest gift of heaven and the highest treasure of earth.

We believe in the immortality and the ongoing of the soul. Man is an embodiment of the living God. Something Divine and eternal has entered into and will never depart from him. And all men are immortal. We could not believe that one person is immortal while another is not. We cannot, with intelligence, believe that any profession of faith or confession of belief has anything to do with eternal Reality. When everyone believed that the world was flat, it was still round. And some day we shall have the grace to know that every person, no matter what his belief, no matter what his conviction, is some part, some embodiment of the living Spirit, that the Divine essence in him, which is God, must be and is as eternal as God himself.

We go from this world into another, and That which is us, being immortal, being eternal, goes on, carrying with it everything that makes for the warmth and color and responsiveness of human personality. Just as when we entered this world we were met by loving friends and tender care, so in the next we have every right to believe the same condition will attend us.

> And with the morn
> Those angel faces smile
> Which I have loved long since,
> And lost awhile.

It is merely this physical body, this physical instrument that passes away, this thing that disintegrates with death. That which makes for the warmth, the color and responsiveness of the person himself, That which responds to us, and That to which we respond, is as eternal, as everlasting as Reality Itself.

This is the belief that the great, the good and the wise of all the ages have held: that all men are on the pathway of an eternal destiny, a destiny which is being painted by invisible brush strokes, every minute of the day.

There is one Life, that Life is God, that Life has given of Itself equally, impartially and impersonally to each one of us, and that which Life has given It will not take away or destroy.

But someone might say: How can this be, since we have not seen the mind, the soul, or the spirit? As a matter of fact, what have we really seen? No biologist has seen life, yet he studies the action and reaction of this invisible and illusive thing that he calls "life." No man has seen life, nor has any physicist seen energy. He cannot say that it looks like this, or that, or something else, and yet he deals with that energy which is in, through, and around all things. We might say of that energy as we do of the Spirit: "In him (or it) we live, and move, and have our being." There is an infinite sea of living energy that no physicist has seen, yet he deals with it and believes in it.

Nor has any psychologist seen the mind, that subtle and illusive thing without which we could not even be aware of our own existence. Where is it? What is it? What does it look like? You cannot isolate the mind; you cannot say it is in the brain or the fingers or the feet. Yet it is the mind and its action and reaction with which the psychologist deals. Nor has any artist seen beauty. He cannot say it "looks like" this or that, nor can he weigh or measure it. He feels it, and out of that feeling he creates the object of art which is a manifestation of his own inward subjective feeling. Who could doubt that beauty exists? Because the beautiful proclaims its own existence.

No! We have not seen God at any time, but the Son has revealed the Father. That is, we know there is Life back of our living or we could not be alive; in Him we do live and move and have our being. And truly He has some part of His being in us.

Every man is an individualized portion of creative Life. The life we express on this plane is but a projection of the Invisible. The process never shows its face, but we know that behind this life is the thinker, the doer, the knower; that which is eternal, that which alone exists. We live because God lives in us. Not I, "but the Father that dwelleth in me, he doeth the works." And when, by reason of any fact, this physical body is no longer a fit instrument for the soul, then the soul quietly lays it aside and we pass to inherit a residence afresh.

As we think back on the lives of those we have loved and lost, just for a while, we should loose them and let them go into the larger life, into the greater good, into that Divine and Perfect Presence which encompasses man here, there, and everywhere; loose them in joy on the pathway which we ourselves someday will follow.

Sunset and evening star
And one clear call for me,
And may there be no moaning of the bar
When I put out to sea,

But such a tide as moving seems asleep,
Too full for sound and foam,
When that which drew from out the boundless deep
Turns again home.

Twilight and evening bell,
And after that the dark!
And may there be no sadness of farewell,
When I embark;

For though from out our bourne of Time and Place
The flood may bear me far,
I hope to see my Pilot face to face
When I have crossed the bar.

Man is born of eternal day, not because he wills or wishes it, not because he labors or strives toward it, not because he earns it as a reward, but simply because the Spirit has breathed life into him. And the Spirit which has breathed this life into him has breathed Its own Life and cannot unbreathe It or take It away. If we would only let go of our theological nonsense and let our soul commune with the Universe, it would tell us all these things because we already know them inwardly.

All men are embodiments of God and the soul can no more be lost than God could be lost. What more can life demand of us than that we do the best we know, always trying to improve. And when we do this we shall have done well indeed, and all will be right with our souls, both here and hereafter.

It is logical to suppose that our place in the next life will be what we have made it, a continuation of this, and that we shall be free to work out our own progress, not with fear or trembling, but with peace and in confidence. We should look forward to the future estate as a place where there will be activity and interest, as a place where we shall be in greater harmony with the Divine Law of Life because of a better understanding of It.

Death loses its sting and the grave its victory when we realize that life is eternal. We are not permitted to stay too long in any one place, just long enough to gather the experience necessary to the unfolding and advancement of the soul. This is wise, for should we stay here too long we would become too set, too rigid, too inflexible.

In the process of evolution change is inevitable, and when this change comes we should welcome it with a smile on the lips and a song in the heart. While it is true that we weep for our friends, we should know that their life goes on.

We are thinking, then, of eternity from this larger viewpoint, as a continuity of time, ever and ever expanding, until "time" as we now know and experience it shall be no more. Realizing this, we should see in everyone a budding genius, a becoming God, an unfolding soul, an eternal destiny. As Robert Browning said:

> Grow old along with me!
> The best is yet to be,
> The last of life, for which the first was made:
> Our times are in His hand
> Who saith "A whole I planned,
> Youth shows but half; trust God: see all, nor be afraid!"

> . . . "Praise be Thine!
> I see the whole design,
> I, who saw Power, see now Love perfect too:
> Perfect I call Thy plan:
> Thanks that I was a man!
> Maker, remake, complete,—I trust what Thou shalt do!"

> Therefore I summon age
> To grant youth's heritage,
> Life's struggle having so far reached its term:
> Thence shall I pass, approved
> A man, for ay removed
> From the developed brute; a God though in the germ.

> And I shall thereupon
> Take rest, ere I be gone
> Once more on my adventure brave and new:
> Fearless and unperplexed,
> When I wage battle next,
> What weapons to select, what armour to indue.

> . . . All that is, at all,
> Lasts ever, past recall;
> Earth changes, but thy soul and God stand sure;
> What entered into thee,
> That was, is, and shall be:
> Time's wheel runs back or stops: Potter and clay endure.

Throughout the ages this is what the great have believed in and taught: the immortality of the individual soul, the ongoingness of the individual life. Now, fortunately indeed, this deep spiritual perception, this intuition of the Divine, at long last has been proved to be true. Not only has this been proved, it has also been adequately demonstrated to those who have taken the time and made the effort to inquire, that discarnate spirits have communicated with those still living in this earthly body.

It is no wonder that the Apostle said: "Beloved, now are we the sons of God, and it doth not yet appear what we shall be; but we know that, when he shall appear, we shall be like him; for we shall see him as he is."

This is no different from saying that we are the sons of God right now, this moment; and when He, that is, the Spiritual Man, shall appear, and we recognize Him, we shall be like Him, and we shall see Him as He is.

Jesus said to the thief who died with him on another cross: "Today shalt thou be with me in paradise." In the thought of Jesus there was no long, intermediate waiting; rather, we pass from this life directly into the next, we sleep to this plane and wake to the next.

So we can say of any friend who has passed:

> He is not dead, he is just away
> With a cheery smile and a wave of the hand;
> He has wandered into an unknown land
> And left us dreaming how very fair
> It must be now, since he lingers there.
> So think of him just the same, and say
> He is not dead, he is just away. —**James Whitcomb**

We came from God and to God we shall return. Our friends who have gone are but a short time before us. Already united with those they love, they are conscious, alive, awake and aware. Let us then rejoice that we know these things, and let us thank God that we have witness to their reality.

O glorious dawn, O day most bright,
Across the darkness of earth's night
There comes a shaft of heavenly light,

Shattering darkness from the gloom:
Empty now the narrow room,
The dead has risen from the tomb.

Let us with him awake from sleep,
While deep within cries unto deep,
And heaven and earth their vigil keep.

Awake with him and be reborn
To greet the light of early morn
And live in God's eternal dawn.

From out the tomb's still narrow prison,
The soul immortal now has risen
From out the grave wherein he lay
To God's complete and perfect day.

The light of that first Easter morn
Within our souls shall be reborn
And gently lead o'er land and sea
To where thy many mansions be.

The spirit which came with us from the Invisible constitutes the one great reality of our being. Its ongoingness at the end of this life is all that matters. The soul is the only triumphant, deathless, and unconquerable thing we possess, nor can we doubt that we take it with us into the larger life, for into that life we must take everything that makes us what we really are, everything that is worthwhile; everything that is real here will be real there. "As above so beneath, as below so above; what is true on one plane is true on all." "In my Father's house are many mansions. . . ."

It is the spirit, the mind, the soul, the intelligence, that part of us which is nonphysical, that enters the larger life. As the Prophet said: "Or ever the silver cord be loosed, or the golden bowl be broken, or the pitcher be broken at the fountain, or the wheel broken at the cistern. Then shall the dust return to the earth as it was: and the spirit shall return unto God who gave it."

> Our birth is but a sleep and a forgetting:
> The Soul that rises with us, our life's Star,
>> Hath had elsewhere its setting
>> And cometh from afar:
>> Not in entire forgetfulness,
>> And not in utter nakedness,
> But trailing clouds of glory do we come
>> From God, who is our home.

The universe in which we live is a spiritual system governed by laws that are beneficent. All persons are dear to the heart of the Eternal, and everyone is an incarnation of the living Spirit. When both the fear of life and the fear of death shall have departed from us, and we are no longer afraid of the universe in which we live, we shall discover by some Divine interior awareness that the soul is immortal, forever expanding, forever outgoing, and forever upward spiraling.

It is only because we have been taught to be afraid of the universe that we have questioned that "good shall come at last alike to all." We should think of passing from this world as a great adventure. We should live as though the day in which we live were eternity itself. We should live as children whose hands are placed in the hands of an infinite Protector, children who know that no evil shall befall them, and we should not be afraid of the future.

> Build thee more stately mansions, O my soul,
> As the swift seasons roll!
> Leave thy low-vaulted past!
> Let each new temple, nobler than the last,
> Shut thee from heaven with a dome more vast,
> Till thou at length art free,
> Leaving thine outgrown shell by life's unresting sea!

Yes, we should think of our friends as though they had but started on a greater journey into a larger life, carrying with them everything that makes for the warmth, the color and the responsiveness of human personality. They are not less, but more themselves.

> They are not dead.
> Those we have fondled to our breast
> Have found sweet peace and quiet rest;
> They live and move among the bless'd.

They are not dead.
Beyond earth's slowly setting sun
Another life has just begun;
Another course of action run.

They are not dead.
Beyond earth's storms and mists and rain
Beyond all sorrow, fear and pain
New life, new joy, shall spring again.

They are not dead.
They have but found new songs to sing,
New life and laughter there to bring
To love's eternal spring.

Let us, then, ever seek the consolation of conscious communion with the Divine, ineffable Spirit, the eternal Presence in whose embrace our beloved friends have more intimately drawn. Let us come as children of light into that Light which knows no darkness, as an offspring of life into that Life which knows no death. With peace and confidence, let us lay the memories of the beloved ones who have passed before us on the altar of our high faith, grateful and thankful for lives well lived and well loved. Let us treasure up as sweet rosemary the memory of those who have been so near and dear to us, knowing that today they walk in the garden of God and waft back to us a kiss of love.

And may the light of eternal love and peace and joy be and abide with them, and all the gladness that there is in the universe be with those they have left behind. And may the Love of the great God gather us all together in blessedness and in peace, forever and forever more. *Amen.*

The Psalm of Psalms

The earth is the Lord's
>and the fulness thereof;
>the world,
>and they that dwell therein.
For he hath founded it upon the seas,
>and established it upon the floods.

Lift up your heads,
>O ye gates;
>and be ye lifted up,
>ye everlasting doors;
>and the King of glory shall come in.
Lift up your heads,
>O ye gates;
>even lift them up,
>ye everlasting doors;
>and the King of glory shall come in.
Who is this King of glory?
>The Lord of hosts,
>He is the King of glory.

O Lord our Lord,
>how excellent is thy name
>in all the earth!
>thy glory is above the heavens.
When I consider thy heavens,
>the work of thy fingers,
>the moon and the stars,
>which thou hast ordained;
What is man,
>that thou art mindful of him?
>and the son of man,
>that thou visitest him?
For thou hast made him a little lower than the angels,
>and hast crowned him with glory and honour.

Bless the Lord
> O my soul,
> and forget not all his benefits:

Who forgiveth all thine iniquities;
> who healeth all thy diseases.

Who redeemeth thy life from destruction;
> who crowneth thee with loving kindness
> and tender mercies;

Who satisfieth thy mouth with good things;
> so that thy youth is renewed
> like the eagle's.

He hath not dealt with us after our sins;
> nor rewarded us according to our iniquities.

For as the heaven
> is high above the earth,
> so great is his mercy
> toward them that fear him.

As far as the east is from the west,
> so far hath he removed our transgressions from us.

Like as a father
> pitieth his children,
> so the Lord
> pitieth them that fear him.

I will praise thee,
> O Lord,
> with my whole heart;
> I will shew forth all thy marvellous works.

I will be glad and rejoice in thee:
> I will sing praise to thy name
> O thou Most High.

That I may shew forth all thy praise
> in the gates of the daughter of Zion:
> I will rejoice in thy salvation.

Lord,
> who shall abide in thy tabernacle?
> who shall dwell
> in thy holy hill?

He that walketh uprightly,

and worketh righteousness,
and speaketh the truth in his heart.

The heavens declare the glory of God;
and the firmament sheweth his handy work.
Day unto day uttereth speech,
and night unto night sheweth knowledge.
There is no speech nor language,
where their voice is not heard.
Their line is gone out through all the earth,
and their words
to the end of the world.
In them hath he set a tabernacle for the sun.
His going forth is from the end of the heaven,
and his circuit
unto the ends of it:
and there is nothing hid
from the heat thereof.

The law of the Lord is perfect,
converting the soul:
the testimony of the Lord is sure,
making wise the simple.
The statutes of the Lord are right,
rejoicing the heart:
the commandment of the Lord is pure,
enlightening the eyes.

Let the words of my mouth,
and the meditation of my heart,
be acceptable in thy sight,
O Lord, my strength, and my redeemer.

One thing have I desired of the Lord,
that will I seek after;
that I may dwell in the house of the Lord
all the days of my life,
to behold the beauty of the Lord,
and to inquire in his temple.

For in the time of trouble
 he shall hide me in his pavilion:
 in the secret of his tabernacle
 shall he hide me;
 he shall set me up
 upon a rock.

The Lord is my strength and my shield;
 my heart trusted in him, and I am helped:
 therefore my heart greatly rejoiceth;
 and with my song will I praise him.

The word of the Lord is right;
 and all his works are done in truth.
By the word of the Lord were the heavens made;
 and all the host of them
 by the breath of his mouth.
For he spake,
 and it was done;
 he commanded,
 and it stood fast.

How excellent is thy loving-kindness, O God!
 Therefore the children of men
 put their trust
 under the shadow of thy wings.
They shall be abundantly satisfied
 with the fatness of thy house;
 and thou shalt make them drink
 of the river of thy pleasures.
For with thee is the fountain of life:
 in thy light shall we see light.

Trust in the Lord,
 and do good;
 so shalt thou dwell in the land,
 and verily thou shalt be fed.
Delight thyself also in the Lord;
 and he shall give thee

the desires of thine heart.
Commit thy way unto the Lord;
    trust also in him;
    and he shall bring it to pass.

My soul, wait thou only upon God;
    for my expectation is from him:
He only is my rock and my salvation:
    he is my defence;
    I shall not be moved.
In God is my salvation and my glory:
    the rock of my strength,
    and my refuge,
    is in God.
For thou, Lord, art good,
    and ready to forgive;
    and plenteous in mercy
    unto all them that call upon thee.
Among the gods there is none like unto thee,
    O Lord;
    neither are there any works like unto thy works.
For thou art great,
    and doest wondrous things:
    thou art God alone.

Teach me thy way,
    O Lord;
    I will walk in thy truth:
I will praise thee,
    O Lord my God,
    with all my heart:
    and I will glorify thy name for evermore.
I will sing of the mercies of the Lord for ever:
    with my mouth
    will I make known thy faithfulness
to all generations.

O Lord God of hosts,
    who is a strong Lord like unto thee?

The heavens are thine,
 the earth also is thine:
 as for the world and the fulness thereof,
 thou hast founded them.
Justice and judgment
 are the habitation of thy throne:
 mercy and truth
 shall go before thy face.

Blessed is the people that know the joyful sound:
 they shall walk,
 O Lord,
 in the light of thy countenance.
In thy name shall they rejoice
 all the day:
 and in thy righteousness
 shall they be exalted.

Lord, thou hast been our dwelling-place
 in all generations.
Before the mountains were brought forth,
 or ever thou hadst formed the earth and the world,
 even from everlasting to everlasting,
 thou art God.
For a thousand years
 in thy sight
 are but as yesterday when it is past,
 and as a watch in the night.
So teach us to number our days,
 that we may apply our hearts unto wisdom.
Surely his salvation is nigh them that fear him;
 that glory may dwell in our land.
Mercy and truth are met together;
 righteousness and peace
 have kissed each other.
Truth shall spring out of the earth;
 and righteousness shall look down from heaven.
O Lord, how great are thy works!
 and thy thoughts are very deep.

He that planted the ear,
    shall he not hear?
    he that formed the eye,
    shall he not see?
Unless the Lord had been my help,
    my soul had almost dwelt in silence.
When I said,
    My foot slippeth;
    thy mercy, O Lord,
    held me up.
The Lord is my defence;
    and my God is the rock of my refuge.
Bless the Lord, O my soul.
    O Lord my God,
    thou art very great;
    thou art clothed with honour and majesty.
Who coverest thyself with light
    as with a garment:
    who stretchest out the heavens
    like a curtain:
Who layeth the beams of his chambers in the waters:
    who maketh the clouds his chariot:
    who walketh upon the wings of the wind:
Who maketh his angels spirits;
    his ministers a flaming fire.

I will sing unto the Lord
    as long as I live:
I will sing praise to my God
    while I have my being.
My meditation of him shall be sweet:
    I will be glad in the Lord.
Seek the Lord, and his strength:
    seek his face evermore.
O God, my heart is fixed;
    I will sing and give praise,
    even with my glory.

Blessed is the man

that walketh not in the counsel of the ungodly.
But his delight is in the law of the Lord;
    and in his law doth he meditate
    day and night.
And he shall be like a tree
    planted by the rivers of water,
    that bringeth forth his fruit in his season;
    his leaf also shall not wither;
    and whatsoever he doeth shall prosper.

I cried unto the Lord with my voice,
    and he heard me
    out of his holy hill.
I laid me down and slept;
    I awaked;
    for the Lord sustained me.
Thou hast put gladness in my heart.
I will both lay me down in peace, and sleep:
    for thou, Lord,
    makest me to dwell in safety.

Let all those that put their trust in thee rejoice:
    let them ever shout for joy,
    because thou defendest them:
    let them also that love thy name
    be joyful in thee.
For thou, Lord, wilt bless the righteous;
    with favor
    wilt thou compass him
    as with a shield.
The Lord is the portion of mine inheritance
    and of my cup:
    thou maintainest my lot.
The lines are fallen unto me in pleasant places;
    yea, I have a goodly heritage.
I have set the Lord always before me:
    because he is at my right hand,
    I shall not be moved.
Therefore my heart is glad,

and my glory rejoiceth:
    my flesh also shall rest in hope.

Thou wilt shew me the path of life:
    in thy presence is fulness of joy;
    at thy right hand there are pleasures
    for evermore.
As for me,
    I will behold thy face in righteousness:
    I shall be satisfied,
    when I awake, with thy likeness.

How amiable are thy tabernacles,
    O Lord of hosts!
My soul longeth,
    yea, even fainteth
    for the courts of the Lord:
    my heart and my flesh
    crieth out for the living God.
Yea, the sparrow hath found an house,
    and the swallow a nest for herself,
    where she may lay her young,
    even thine altars,
    O Lord of hosts, My King, and my God.
For a day in thy courts
    is better than a thousand.
    I had rather be a doorkeeper
    in the house of my God,
    than to dwell in the tents of wickedness.

The Lord God is a sun and shield:
    the Lord will give grace and glory;
    no good thing will he withhold
    from them that walk uprightly.
O Lord of Hosts,
    blessed is the man that trusteth in thee.
They that trust in the Lord
    shall be as mount Zion,
    which cannot be removed,

but abideth for ever.

As the mountains are round about Jerusalem,
    so the Lord is round about his people
    from henceforth even for ever.
Behold, bless ye the Lord,
    all ye servants of the Lord,
    which by night stand in the house of the Lord.
Lift up your hands in the sanctuary,
    and bless the Lord.
The Lord that made heaven and earth,
    bless thee out of Zion.

I will praise thee, O Lord,
    among the people:
    I will sing unto thee
    among the nations.
For thy mercy is great unto the heavens:
    and thy truth
    unto the clouds.
O praise the Lord,
    all ye nations:
    praise him, all ye people.
For his merciful kindness is great toward us:
    and the truth of the Lord endureth for ever.
    Praise ye the Lord.

O give thanks unto the Lord;
    for he is good:
    because his mercy endureth for ever.
Bless the Lord,
    O my soul:
    and all that is within me
    bless his holy name.
Thou openest thine hand,
    and satisfiest the desire of every living thing.

The Lord is righteous
    in all his ways,

and holy in all his works.
The Lord is nigh unto them that call upon him,
      to all that call upon him in truth.

Praise ye the Lord. Praise the Lord,
      O my soul.
While I live will I praise the Lord:
      I will sing praises unto my God
      while I have any being.
Praise ye the Lord,
      praise God in his sanctuary:
      praise him in the firmament of his power.
Let every thing that hath breath
      praise the Lord.
      Praise ye the Lord.

O come,
      let us sing unto the Lord:
      let us make a joyful noise
      to the rock of our salvation.
For he is our God;
      and we are the people of his pasture,
      and the sheep of his hand.

O sing unto the Lord a new song:
      sing unto the Lord,
      all the earth;
Sing unto the Lord,
      bless his name;
      shew forth his salvation from day to day.
Honour and majesty are before him:
      strength and beauty are in his sanctuary.
O worship the Lord
      in the beauty of holiness:
Let the field be joyful,
      and all that is therein:
      then shall all the trees of the wood rejoice.

Rejoice in the Lord,

ye righteous;
and give thanks at the remembrance of his holiness.
Make a joyful noise unto the Lord, all ye lands,
Serve the Lord with gladness:
come before his presence with singing.

Know ye that the Lord he is God:
it is he that hath made us,
and not we ourselves;
we are his people,
and the sheep of his pasture.

Enter into his gates with thanksgiving,
and into his courts with praise:
be thankful unto him, and bless his name.
For the Lord is good;
his mercy is everlasting;
and his truth endureth to all generations.

I will meditate in thy precepts,
and have respect unto thy ways.
I will delight myself in thy statutes:
I will not forget thy word.
Open thou mine eyes,
that I may behold wondrous things
out of thy law.
Thy testimonies also are my delight and my counsellors.

Make me to understand the way of thy precepts:
so shall I talk of thy wondrous works.
Teach me, O Lord, the way of thy statutes;
and I shall keep it unto the end.
Give me understanding,
and I shall keep thy law;
yea, I shall observe it with my whole heart.
And I will delight myself in thy commandments,
which I have loved.
At midnight I will rise to give thanks unto thee
because of thy righteous judgments.

The earth, O Lord,
    is full of thy mercy:
    teach me thy statutes.
For ever
    O Lord,
    thy word is settled in heaven.
Thy faithfulness is unto all generations:
    thou hast established the earth,
    and it abideth.
O how I love thy law!
    it is my meditation all the day.
Thou art my hiding place and my shield:
    I hope in thy word.

Great peace have they which love thy law:
    and nothing shall offend them.
My lips shall utter praise,
    when thou hast taught me thy statutes.
My tongue shall speak of thy word:
    for all thy commandments are righteousness.

As the hart panteth after the water brooks,
    so panteth my soul after thee, O God.
My soul thirsteth for God,
    for the living God:

Why art thou cast down, O my soul?
    and why art thou disquieted in me?
    Hope thou in God:
    for I shall yet praise him
    for the help of his countenance.
God is our refuge and strength,
    a very present help in trouble.
Therefore will not we fear,
    though the earth be removed,
    and though the mountains
    be carried into the midst of the sea.

There is a river,

the streams whereof
shall make glad
the city of God,
the holy place
of the tabernacles
of the Most High.
The Lord is my strength and song,
and is become my salvation.
I shall not die
but live,
and declare the works of the Lord.
Open to me the gates of righteousness:
I will go into them,
and I will praise the Lord:
This is the day which the Lord hath made;
we will rejoice and be glad in it.

Thou art my God,
and I will praise thee:
thou art my God,
I will exalt thee.
O give thanks unto the Lord;
for he is good:
for his mercy endureth for ever.

He that dwelleth
in the secret place of the Most High
shall abide
under the shadow
of the Almighty.

I will say of the Lord,
He is my refuge and my fortress:
my God;
in him will I trust.
Surely he shall deliver thee
from the snare of the fowler,
and from the noisome pestilence.

He shall cover thee with his feathers,
    and under his wings shalt thou trust:
    his truth
    shall be thy shield and buckler.
Thou shalt not be afraid
    for the terror by night;
    nor for the arrow
    that flieth by day;
Nor for the pestilence
    that walketh in darkness;
    nor for the destruction
    that wasteth at noonday.
Because thou hast made the Lord,
    which is my refuge,
    even the Most High,
    thy habitation;
There shall no evil befall thee,
    neither shall any plague come nigh thy dwelling.
For he shall give his angels charge over thee,
    to keep thee
    in all thy ways.
They shall bear thee up in their hands,
    lest thou dash thy foot
    against a stone.
Because he hath set his love upon me,
    therefore will I deliver him:
    I will set him on high,
    because he hath known my name.
He shall call upon me,
    and I will answer him:
    I will be with him in trouble;
    I will deliver him and honour him.
With long life will I satisfy him,
    and shew him my salvation.

I will extol thee,
    my God;
    and I will bless thy name for ever and ever.
Every day will I bless thee;

and I will praise thy name
for ever and ever.

The Lord is gracious,
and full of compassion.
Thy kingdom is an everlasting kingdom,
and thy dominion
endureth throughout all generations.

I will lift up mine eyes
unto the hills,
from whence cometh my help.
My help cometh from the Lord,
which made heaven and earth.
He will not suffer thy foot to be moved:
he that keepeth thee
will not slumber.
Behold,
he that keepeth Israel
shall neither slumber nor sleep.

The Lord is thy keeper:
the Lord is thy shade
upon thy right hand.
The sun shall not smite thee by day,
nor the moon by night.
The Lord shall preserve thee from all evil:
he shall preserve thy soul.
The Lord shall preserve thy going out and thy coming in
from this time forth
and even for evermore.

Our soul is escaped
as a bird out of the snare of the fowlers:
the snare is broken,
and we are escaped.
Our help is in the name of the Lord,
who made heaven and earth.
For thou hast delivered my soul from death,

mine eyes from tears,
and my feet from falling.

Whither shall I go from thy Spirit?
or whither shall I flee from thy presence?
If I ascend up into heaven,
thou art there:
if I make my bed in hell,
behold,
thou art there.
If I take the wings of the morning,
and dwell in the uttermost parts of the sea;
Even there shall thy hand lead me,
and thy right hand shall hold me.

The Lord is my shepherd;
I shall not want.

He maketh me to lie down in green pastures:
he leadeth me beside the still waters.
He restoreth my soul:
he leadeth me in the paths of righteousness
for his name's sake.
Yea, though I walk through the valley
of the shadow of death,
I will fear no evil:
for thou art with me;
thy rod and thy staff they comfort me.
Thou preparest a table before me
in the presence of mine enemies:
thou anointest my head with oil;
my cup runneth over.
Surely goodness and mercy
shall follow me all the days of my life:
and I will dwell in the house of the Lord
for ever.

The Wisdom of Solomon

My son, hear the instruction of thy father,
>and forsake not the law of thy mother:
A wise man will hear,
>and will increase learning;
>and a man of understanding
>shall attain unto wise counsels:
The fear of the Lord is the beginning of knowledge:
>but fools despise wisdom and instruction.
For they shall be an ornament of grace unto thy head,
>and chains about thy neck.

Wisdom crieth without;
>she uttereth her voice in the streets;
She crieth in the chief place of concourse,
>in the openings of the gates:
>in the city
>she uttereth her words.
Incline thine ear
>unto wisdom,
>and apply thine heart
>to understanding;
Whoso hearkeneth unto me
>shall dwell safely,
>and shall be quiet
>from fear of evil.

For the Lord giveth wisdom:
>out of his mouth
>cometh knowledge and understanding.
He layeth up sound wisdom
>for the righteous:
>he is a buckler
>to them that walk uprightly.

Happy is the man that findeth wisdom,

and the man that getteth understanding.
For the merchandise of it
    is better than the merchandise of silver,
    and the gain thereof
    than fine gold.
She is more precious than rubies:
    and all the things thou canst desire
    are not to be compared unto her.
Length of days is in her right hand;
    and in her left hand,
    riches and honour.
Her ways are ways of pleasantness,
    and all her paths are peace.

Forget not my law,
    but let thine heart
    keep my commandments:
For length of days,
    and long life, and peace,
    shall they add to thee.
For they are life unto those that find them,
    and health to all their flesh.

Keep thy heart with all diligence;
    for out of it are the issues of life.
My son, keep thy father's commandment,
    and forsake not the law of thy mother:
Bind them continually upon thine heart,
    and tie them about thy neck.
Say unto wisdom,
    Thou art my sister;
    and call understanding thy kinswoman.

Get wisdom, get understanding:
    forget it not;
    neither decline from the words of my mouth.
Forsake her not,
    and she shall preserve thee:
    love her, and she shall keep thee.

Wisdom is the principal thing;
>therefore get wisdom:
>and with all thy getting, get understanding.

Exalt her,
>and she shall promote thee:
>she shall bring thee to honour,
>when thou dost embrace her.

She shall give to thine head an ornament of grace:
>a crown of glory shall she deliver to thee.

How much better is it to get wisdom than gold!
>and understanding
>is rather to be chosen than silver!

The Lord by wisdom hath founded the earth;
>by understanding hath he established the heavens.

By his knowledge the depths are broken up,
>and the clouds drop down the dew.

The fear of the Lord is the beginning of wisdom:
>and the knowledge of the holy is understanding.

The wise in heart shall be called prudent:
>and the sweetness of the lips increaseth learning.

Understanding is a well-spring of life
>unto him that hath it:
>but the instruction of fools is folly.

The heart of the wise teacheth his mouth,
>and addeth learning to his lips.

My son, keep my words,
>and lay up my commandments with thee.

Keep my commandments, and live;
>and my law, as the apple of thine eye.

Let not mercy and truth forsake thee:
>bind them about thy neck;
>write them upon the table of thine heart:

Trust in the Lord with all thine heart;
>and lean not unto thine own understanding.

In all thy ways acknowledge him,
>and he shall direct thy paths.

Commit thy works unto the Lord,
    and thy thoughts shall be established.
For the Lord shall be thy confidence,
    and shall keep thy foot from being taken.
When thou liest down,
        thou shalt not be afraid;
        yea, thou shalt lie down,
        and thy sleep shall be sweet.
When thou goest,
        it shall lead thee;
        when thou sleepest,
        it shall keep thee,
        and when thou awakest,
        it shall talk with thee.

My son, if thou receiveth my words,
    and hide my commandments with thee;
Yea, if thou criest after knowledge,
    and liftest up thy voice for understanding;
If thou seekest her as silver,
        and searchest for her
        as for hid treasures;
Then shalt thou understand,
    and find the knowledge of God.
Then shalt thou understand righteousness,
        and judgment, and equity;
        yea, every good path.

Doth not wisdom cry out?
    and understanding put forth her voice?
She standeth in high places,
She crieth at the gates,
        at the entry of the city,
        at the coming in at the doors:
Unto you, O men, I call;
    and my voice is to the sons of man.
O ye simple, understand wisdom:
    and be ye of an understanding heart.
Hear;

for I will speak of excellent things;
and the opening of my lips shall be right things.

Give instruction to a wise man,
and he will be yet wiser:
teach a just man,
and he will increase in learning.
He that getteth wisdom loveth his own soul:
he that keepeth understanding shall find good.
For by me thy days shall be multiplied,
and the years of thy life shall be increased.

Blessed is the man that heareth me,
watching daily at my gates,
waiting at the posts of my doors.
For whoso findeth me findeth life,
and shall obtain favour of the Lord.
The path of the just is as the shining light,
that shineth more and more unto the perfect day.

Wisdom is better than rubies;
and all the things that may be desired
are not to be compared to it.

Counsel is mine
and sound wisdom:
I am understanding;
I have strength.
By me kings reign,
and princes decree justice.
By me princes rule, and nobles,
even all the judges of the earth.

I love them that love me;
and those that seek me early shall find me.
Riches and honour are with me;
yea, durable riches and righteousness.
My fruit is better than gold,
yea, than fine gold;

and my revenue than choice silver.
Apply thine heart unto instruction,
and thine ears to the words of knowledge.
Hearken unto thy father that begat thee,
and despise not thy mother when she is old.

Buy the truth, and sell it not;
Through wisdom is an house builded;
and by understanding it is established:
By knowledge shall the chambers be filled
with all precious and pleasant riches.
A wise man is strong;
yea, a man of knowledge increaseth strength.

My son, eat thou honey,
because it is good;
and the honeycomb,
which is sweet to thy taste:
So shall the knowledge of wisdom be unto thy soul:
when thou hast found it,
then there shall be a reward,
and thy expectation shall not be cut off.
Hear counsel, and receive instruction,
that thou mayest be wise in thy latter days.
There are many devices in a man's heart;
nevertheless the counsel of the Lord,
that shall stand.
Counsel in the heart of man is like deep water;
but a man of understanding
will draw it out.

The just man walketh in his integrity:
his children are blessed after him.
There is gold,
and a multitude of rubies:
but the lips of knowledge are a precious jewel.
So shall they be life unto thy soul,
and grace to thy neck.

Then shalt thou walk in thy way safely,
    and thy foot shall not stumble.

Hear, O my son,
    and receive my sayings;
    and the years of thy life shall be many.
I have taught thee in the way of wisdom;
    I have led thee in right paths.
When thou goest,
    thy steps shall not be straitened;
    and when thou runnest,
    thou shalt not stumble.
Take fast hold of instruction;
    let her not go:
    keep her;
    for she is thy life.

When a man's ways please the Lord,
    he maketh even his enemies
    to be at peace with him.
Pride goeth before destruction,
    and an haughty spirit before a fall.
Better it is to be of an humble spirit with the lowly,
    than to divide the spoil with the proud.
Better is a little with righteousness
    than great revenues without right.
Better is little with the fear of the Lord
    than great treasure and trouble therewith.
Better is a dinner of herbs where love is
    than a stalled ox and hatred therewith.

The name of the Lord is a strong tower:
    the righteous runneth into it,
    and is safe.
A man that hath friends must shew himself friendly:
    and there is a friend that sticketh
    closer than a brother.
A good name is rather to be chosen than great riches,
    and loving favour

rather than silver and gold.

Boast not thyself of tomorrow;
for thou knowest not what a day may bring forth.
Let another man praise thee,
and not thine own mouth;
a stranger, and not thine own lips.

If thine enemy be hungry, give him bread to eat;
and if he be thirsty,
give him water to drink:
For thou shalt heap coals of fire upon his head,
and the Lord shall reward thee.

Cast thy bread upon the waters:
for thou shalt find it after many days.

The eyes of the Lord are in every place,
beholding the evil and the good.
Whoso rewardeth evil for good,
evil shall not depart from his house.
He that diggeth a pit shall fall into it;
and whoso breaketh an hedge,
a serpent shall bite him.
It is better to hear the rebuke of the wise,
than for a man to hear the song of fools.

Be not hasty in thy spirit to be angry:
for anger resteth in the bosom of fools.
A wise man scaleth the city of the mighty,
and casteth down the strength
of the confidence thereof.

He that answereth a matter before he heareth it,
it is folly and shame unto him.
The heart of the prudent getteth knowledge;
and the ear of the wise seeketh knowledge.

As the whirlwind passeth,

so is the wicked no more:
but the righteous is an everlasting foundation.
The wise in heart will receive commandments:
He that walketh uprightly walketh surely:
To do justice and judgment
is more acceptable to the Lord than sacrifice.

The Lord possessed me in the beginning of his way,
before his works of old.
I was set up from everlasting,
from the beginning,
or ever the earth was.
When there were no depths,
I was brought forth;
when there were no fountains
abounding with water.

A man's heart deviseth his way:
but the Lord directeth his steps.
A merry heart maketh a cheerful countenance:
but by sorrow the spirit is broken.
The heart of him that hath understanding
seeketh knowledge:
but the mouth of fools feedeth on foolishness.
All the days of the afflicted are evil:
but he that is of a merry heart hath a continual feast.

Give not sleep to thine eyes,
nor slumber to thine eyelids.
Go to the ant, thou sluggard;
consider her ways and be wise;
Which having no guide, overseer, or ruler,
provideth her meat in the summer,
and gathereth her food in the harvest.
How long wilt thou sleep,
O sluggard?
when wilt thou arise out of thy sleep?

A wise son maketh a glad father:

but a foolish son is the heaviness of his mother.
He becometh poor that dealeth with a slack hand:
     but the hand of the diligent maketh rich.
He that gathereth in summer is a wise son:
     but he that sleepeth in harvest causeth shame.

The hope of the righteous shall be gladness:
The way of the Lord is strength to the upright:
The righteous shall never be removed:
Where no counsel is, the people fall:
     but in the multitude of counsellors there is safety.
Where there is no vision,
     the people perish:
     but he that keepeth the law,
     happy is he.

The man that wandereth out of the way of understanding
     shall remain in the congregation of the dead.
He that followeth after righteousness and mercy
     findeth life, righteousness and honour.
Lo, this only have I found,
     that God hath made man upright;
     but they have sought out many inventions.

Wilt thou set thine eyes upon that which is not?
     for riches certainly make themselves wings;
     they fly away as an eagle toward heaven.
There is that scattereth,
     and yet increaseth;
The liberal soul shall be made fat:
     and he that watereth
     shall be watered.

The merciful man doeth good to his own soul:
     but he that is cruel troubleth his own flesh.
Eat thou not the bread of him that is evil,
     neither desire thou his dainty meats:
Can a man take fire in his bosom,
     and his clothes not be burned?

The mouth of the just bringeth forth wisdom:
The lips of the righteous know what is acceptable:
>   but the mouth of the wicked speaketh forwardness.
A man hath joy by the answer of his mouth:
>   and a word spoken in due season, how good is it!
When pride cometh, then cometh shame:
>   but with the lowly is wisdom.
The integrity of the upright shall guide them:
By the blessing of the upright
>   the city is exalted:
>   but it is overthrown
>   by the mouth of the wicked.
He that is void of wisdom despiseth his neighbour:
>   but a man of understanding holdeth his peace.

The spirit of man is the candle of the Lord,
The lip of truth
>   shall be established for ever;
>   but a lying tongue is but for a moment.

Deceit is in the heart of them that imagine evil:
>   but to the counsellors of peace is joy.
Heaviness in the heart of man maketh it stoop:
>   but a good word maketh it glad.
The way of a fool is right in his own eyes:
>   but he that hearkeneth unto counsel is wise.

A fool's mouth is his destruction,
>   and his lips are the snare of his soul.
The tongue of the just is as choice silver:
>   the heart of the wicked is little worth.
A wholesome tongue is a tree of life:
>   but perverseness therein is a breach in the spirit.
Righteous lips are the delight of kings;
>   and they love him that speaketh right.
Whoso keepeth his mouth and his tongue
>   keepeth his soul from troubles.
Death and life are in the power of the tongue
>   and they that love it shall eat the fruit thereof.

Pleasant words are as an honeycomb,
    sweet to the soul,
    and health to the bones.
The words of a man's mouth are as deep waters,
    and the wellspring of wisdom as a flowing brook.
A word fitly spoken
    is like apples of gold in pictures of silver.

As an earring of gold,
    and an ornament of fine gold,
    so is a wise reprover upon an obedient ear.
Hope deferred maketh the heart sick:
    but when the desire cometh,
    it is a tree of life.
A soft answer turneth away wrath:
    but grievous words stir up anger.
The tongue of the wise useth knowledge aright:
    but the mouth of fools poureth out foolishness

The mouth of a righteous man is a well of life:
Hatred stirreth up strifes:
    but love covereth all sins.
In the lips of him that hath understanding
    wisdom is found:
    but a rod is for the back of him
    that is void of understanding.
Wise men lay up knowledge:
    but the mouth of the foolish is near destruction.
Vanity of vanities,
    saith the Preacher,
    vanity of vanities;
    all is vanity.
One generation passeth away,
    and another generation cometh:
    but the earth abideth for ever.

The thing that hath been,
    it is that which shall be;
    and that which is done

is that which shall be done:

and there is no new thing under the sun.

To every thing there is a season,

and a time to every purpose under the heaven:

A time to be born,

and a time to die;

a time to plant,

and a time to pluck up

that which is planted;

A time to weep, and a time to laugh;

a time to mourn,

and a time to cast away.

I know that, whatsoever God doeth,

it shall be for ever:

nothing can be put to it,

nor any thing taken from it:

That which hath been is now;

and that which is to be

hath already been.

As [man] came forth of his mother's womb,

naked shall he return to go as he came,

and shall take nothing of his labour,

which he may carry away in his hand.

As thou knowest not what is the way of the spirit,

nor how the bones do grow

in the womb of her

that is with child:

even so thou knowest not the works of God

who maketh all.

In the morning sow thy seed,

and in the evening

withhold not thine hand:

for thou knowest not whether shall prosper,

either this or that,

or whether they both shall be alike good.

Remember now thy Creator

in the days of thy youth,

while the evil days come not,
nor the years draw nigh,
when thou shalt say,
I have no pleasure in them;
While the sun,
or the light,
or the moon,
or the stars,
be not darkened,
nor the clouds return
after the rain:
Or ever the silver cord be loosed,
or the golden bowl be broken,
or the pitcher
be broken at the fountain,
or the wheel
broken at the cistern.
Then shall the dust
return to the earth as it was:
and the spirit
shall return unto God who gave it.

The Song of Isaiah

Thus saith the Lord,
    The heaven is my throne,
    and the earth is my footstool;
For all those things hath mine hand made.
Come now,
    and let us reason together,
    saith the Lord:
    though your sins be as scarlet,
    they shall be as white as snow;
    though they be red like crimson,
    they shall be as wool.
For, behold,
    I create new heavens and a new earth:
    and the former shall not be remembered,
    nor come into mind.
Remember ye not the former things,
    neither consider the things of old.
Behold, I will do a new thing;
    now it shall spring forth;
    I will even make a way in the wilderness,
    and rivers in the desert.
I, even I, am he that blotteth out thy transgressions
    for mine own sake,
    and will not remember thy sins.

For thus saith the Lord God,
    the Holy One of Israel;
    In returning and rest
    shall ye be saved;
    in quietness and in confidence
    shall be your strength:
And thine ears shall hear a word behind thee,
    saying, This is the way,
    walk ye in it,
    when ye turn to the right hand,

and when ye turn to the left.

The wilderness and the solitary place
     shall be glad;
     and the desert shall rejoice,
     and blossom as the rose.
It shall blossom abundantly,
     and rejoice even with joy and singing:
     the glory of Lebanon shall be given unto it,
     the excellency of Carmel and Sharon:
     they shall see the glory of the Lord,
     and the excellency of our God.

Strengthen ye the weak hands,
     and confirm the feeble knees.
Say to them that are of a fearful heart,
     Be strong, fear not:
     behold, your God will come;
     he will come and save you.
Then the eyes of the blind shall be opened,
     and the ears of the deaf shall be unstopped.
Then shall the lame man leap as an hart,
     and the tongue of the dumb sing:
     for in the wilderness
     shall waters break out,
     and streams in the desert.
And the inhabitants shall not say,
     I am sick:
     the people that dwell therein
     shall be forgiven their iniquity.
And the parched ground shall become a pool,
     and the thirsty land springs of water.

And an highway shall be there,
     and a way,
     and it shall be called
     The way of holiness;
     the unclean shall not pass over it;
     the wayfaring men, though fools,

shall not err therein.
No lion shall be there,
    nor any ravenous beast shall go up thereon,
    it shall not be found there; but
    the redeemed shall walk there:
And the ransomed of the Lord shall return,
    and come to Zion with songs
    and everlasting joy upon their heads:
    they shall obtain joy and gladness,
    and sorrow and sighing shall flee away.

Fear not: for I have redeemed thee,
    I have called thee by thy name;
    thou art mine.
When thou passest through the waters,
    I will be with thee;
    and through the rivers,
    they shall not overflow thee:
    when thou walkest through the fire,
    thou shalt not be burned;
    neither shall the flame kindle upon thee.
Fear thou not;
    for I am with thee:
    be not dismayed;
    for I am thy God:
    I will strengthen thee;
    yea, I will help thee;
    yea, I will uphold thee
    with the right hand of my righteousness.

For I the Lord thy God will hold thy right hand,
    saying unto thee,
    Fear not; I will help thee.
I will open rivers in high places,
    and fountains in the midst of the valleys:
    I will make the wilderness a pool of water,
    and the dry land springs of water.
I will plant in the wilderness the cedar,
    and the myrtle, and the oil tree;

I will set in the desert the fir tree,
and the pine, and the box tree together.

And I will bring the blind by a way that they knew not;
I will lead them in paths that they have not known:
I will make darkness light before them,
and crooked things straight.
These things will I do unto them
and not forsake them.

Bring forth the blind people that have eyes,
and the deaf that have ears.
Let all the nations be gathered together,
and let the people be assembled:
Ye are my witnesses,
saith the Lord,
and my servant whom I have chosen:
that ye may know and believe me,
and understand that I am he:
before me there was no God formed.
I, even I, am the Lord;
and beside me there is no saviour.
Yea, before the day was I am he;
and there is none that can deliver out of my hand:
I will work, and who shall let it?

Behold my servant, whom I uphold;
mine elect, in whom my soul delighteth;
I have put my Spirit upon him.
He shall not cry,
nor lift up,
nor cause his voice to be heard in the street.
A bruised reed shall he not break,
and the smoking flax shall he not quench:
he shall bring forth judgment unto truth.

Thus saith God the Lord,
he that created the heavens,
and stretched them out:

he that spread forth the earth,
and that which cometh out of it;
he that giveth breath unto the people upon it,
and spirit to them that walk therein:
I the Lord have called thee in righteousness,
and will hold thine hand,
and will keep thee,
and give thee for a covenant of the people, for a light of the Gentiles;
To open the blind eyes,
to bring out the prisoners from the prison,
and them that sit in darkness
out of the prison house.

I have made the earth,
and created man upon it:
I, even my hands,
have stretched out the heavens,
and all their host have I commanded.
I have raised him up in righteousness,
and I will direct all his ways:
he shall build my city,
and he shall let go my captives,
not for price nor reward,
saith the Lord of hosts.
For thus saith the Lord that created the heavens;
God himself that formed the earth and made it;
he hath established it,
he created it not in vain,
he formed it to be inhabited:
I am the Lord; and there is none else.

Look unto me,
and be ye saved,
all the ends of the earth:
for I am God,
and there is none else.
Mine hand also
hath laid the foundation of the earth,
and my right hand

hath spanned the heavens.

Hearken to me,
    ye that follow after righteousness,
    ye that seek the Lord:
    look unto the rock
    whence ye are hewn,
    and to the hole of the pit
    whence ye are digged.
Hearken unto me, my people;
    and give ear unto me, O my nation:
    for a law shall proceed from me,
    and I will make my judgment to rest
    for a light of the people.
My righteousness is near;
    my salvation is gone forth,
    and mine arms shall judge the people;
    the isles shall wait upon me,
    and on mine arm shall they trust.

I, even I, am he that comforteth you:
    who art thou,
    that thou shouldest be afraid of a man that shall die;
    and of the son of man
    which shall be made as grass;
But I am the Lord thy God,
    that divided the sea,
    whose waves roared.
And I have put my words in thy mouth,
    and I have covered thee
    in the shadow of mine hand,
    that I may plant the heavens,
    and lay the foundations of the earth,
    and say unto Zion,
    Thou art my people.
Therefore my people shall know my name:
    therefore they shall know
    in that day
    that I am he that doth speak:

behold, it is I.

I will pour water upon him that is thirsty,
    and floods upon the dry ground:
    I will pour my Spirit upon thy seed,
    and my blessing upon thine offspring:
I am the first,
    and I am the last;
    and beside me there is no God.
Fear ye not,
    neither be afraid:
    have not I told thee . . . and declared it?
    ye are even my witnesses.
    Is there a God beside me?
    yea, there is no God;
    I know not any.
I will go before thee,
    and make the crooked places straight:
    I will break in pieces the gates of brass,
    and cut in sunder the bars of iron:
And I will give thee the treasures of darkness,
    and hidden riches of secret places,
    that thou mayest know that I,
    the Lord, which call thee by thy name,
    am God.

I am the Lord,
    and there is none else,
    there is no God beside me:
Sing, O heavens;
    and be joyful, O earth;
    and break forth into singing,
O mountains:
    for the Lord hath comforted his people.
How beautiful upon the mountains
    are the feet of him
    that bringeth good tidings,
    that publisheth peace;
    that publisheth salvation;

that saith unto Zion,
Thy God reigneth!
Thy watchmen shall lift up the voice;
with the voice together shall they sing:
for they shall see eye to eye.
Break forth into joy,
sing together,
ye waste places of Jerusalem;
for the Lord hath comforted his people,
he hath redeemed Jerusalem.

The Lord hath made bare his holy arm
in the eyes of all the nations;
and all the ends of the earth
shall see the salvation of our God.
That they may know from the rising of the sun,
and from the west,
that there is none beside me.
I am the Lord, and there is none else.

O Lord, thou art my God;
I will exalt thee,
I will praise thy name;
for thou hast done wonderful things;
thy counsels of old are faithfulness and truth.
For thou hast been a strength to the poor,
a strength to the needy in his distress,
a refuge from the storm,
a shadow from the heat.

Who hath measured the waters in the hollow of his hand,
and meted out heaven with the span,
and comprehended the dust of the earth in a measure,
and weighed the mountains in scales,
and the hills in a balance?
To whom then will ye liken God?
or what likeness will ye compare unto him?
Have ye not known?
have ye not heard?

hath it not been told you
from the beginning?
have ye not understood
from the foundations of the earth?
It is he that sitteth upon the circle of the earth,
　　that stretcheth out the heavens as a curtain,
　　and spreadeth them out as a tent to dwell in.

Lift up your eyes on high,
　　and behold who hath created these things,
　　that bringeth out their host by number:
　　he calleth them all by names
　　by the greatness of his might,
　　for that he is strong in power;
　　not one faileth.
Hast thou not known,
　　hast thou not heard,
　　that the everlasting God,
　　the Lord, the Creator of the ends of the earth,
　　fainteth not,
　　neither is weary?
　　there is no searching of his understanding.
He giveth power to the faint;
　　and to them that have no might he
　　increaseth strength.
Even the youths shall faint and be weary,
　　and the young men shall utterly fall:
But they that wait upon the Lord
　　shall renew their strength;
　　they shall mount up with wings as eagles;
　　they shall run, and not be weary;
　　they shall walk,
　　and not faint.

Ye shall not go out with haste,
　　nor go by flight:
　　f or the Lord will go before you;
　　and the God of Israel
　　will be your rereward.

Ho, every one that thirsteth,
    come ye to the waters,
    and he that hath no money;
    come ye, buy, and eat;
    yea, come, buy wine and milk
    without money
    and without price.
Incline your ear, and come unto me:
    hear, and your soul shall live;
    and I will make an everlasting covenant with you,
    even the sure mercies of David.
Seek ye the Lord while he may be found,
    call ye upon him while he is near;
Let the wicked forsake his way,
    and the unrighteous man his thoughts:
    and let him return unto the Lord,
    and he will have mercy upon him;
    and to our God,
    for he will abundantly pardon.
For my thoughts are not your thoughts,
    neither are your ways my ways,
    saith the Lord.

For as the heavens are higher than the earth,
    so are my ways higher than your ways,
    and my thoughts than your thoughts.
For as the rain cometh down,
    and the snow from heaven,
    and returneth not thither,
    but watereth the earth,
    and maketh it bring forth and bud,
    that it may give seed to the sower,
    and bread to the eater:
So shall my word be that goeth forth out of my mouth:
    it shall not return unto me void,
    but it shall accomplish that which I please, and
    it shall prosper
    in the thing whereto I sent it.
Ye shall go out with joy,

and be led forth with peace:
the mountains and the hills
shall break forth before you
into singing,
and all the trees of the field
shall clap their hands.

Instead of the thorn
shall come up the fir tree,
and instead of the brier
shall come up the myrtle tree;
and it shall be to the Lord for a name,
for an everlasting sign
that shall not be cut off.
Behold, the Lord's hand is not shortened,
that it cannot save;
neither his ear heavy,
that it cannot hear:
As for me, this is my covenant with them,
saith the Lord:
My Spirit that is upon thee,
and my words
which I have put in thy mouth,
shall not depart out of thy mouth,
nor out of the mouth of thy seed,
nor out of the mouth of thy seed's seed.
O thou afflicted,
tossed with tempest, and not comforted,
behold,
I will lay thy stones with fair colours,
and lay thy foundations with sapphires.
And I will make thy windows of agates,
and thy gates of carbuncles,
and all thy borders of pleasant stones.
And all thy children shall be taught of the Lord;
and great shall be the peace of thy children.
In righteousness shalt thou be established:
thou shalt be far from oppression;
for thou shalt not fear:

and from terror;
    for it shall not come near thee.
No weapon that is formed against thee shall prosper;
    and every tongue
    that shall rise against thee in judgment
    thou shalt condemn.
    This is the heritage of the servants of the Lord,
    and their righteousness is of me,
    saith the Lord.

And the eyes of them that see
    shall not be dim,
    and the ears of them that hear
    shall hearken.
The heart also of the rash
    shall understand knowledge,
    and the tongue of the stammerers
    shall be ready to speak plainly.
And the work of righteousness
    shall be peace;
    and the effect of righteousness
    quietness and assurance for ever.
And my people shall dwell in a peaceable habitation,
    and in sure dwellings,
    and in quiet resting places.
Then shall thy light break forth as the morning,
    and thine health shall spring forth speedily:
    and thy righteousness shall go before thee:
    the glory of the Lord shall be thy rereward.
Then shalt thou call,
    and the Lord shall answer;
    thou shalt cry,
    and he shall say, Here I am.

And the Lord shall guide thee continually,
    and satisfy thy soul in drought,
    and make fat thy bones:
    and thou shalt be like a watered garden,
    and like a spring of water,

whose waters fail not.
And a man shall be as an hiding place from the wind,
    and a covert from the tempest;
    as rivers of water in a dry place,
    as the shadow of a great rock in a weary land.

The people that walked in darkness
    have seen a great light:
    they that dwell in the land of the shadow of death,
    upon them hath the light shined.
For unto us a child is born,
    unto us a son is given:
    and the government shall be upon his shoulder:
    and his name shall be called Wonderful, Counsellor,
    The mighty God, The everlasting Father,
    The Prince of Peace.
And the spirit of the Lord shall rest upon him,
    the spirit of wisdom and understanding,
    the spirit of counsel and might,
    the spirit of knowledge
    and of the fear of the Lord;
And shall make him of quick understanding
    in the fear of the Lord:
    and he shall not judge
    after the sight of his eyes,
    neither reprove
    after the hearing of his ears.

Behold, God is my salvation;
    I will trust, and not be afraid:
    for the Lord Jehovah
is my strength and my song;
    he also is become my salvation.
Therefore with joy
    shall ye draw water
    out of the wells of salvation.

For as the earth bringeth forth her bud,

and as the garden causeth the things
that are sown in it
to spring forth;
so the Lord God will cause righteousness and praise
to spring forth before all the nations.
The wolf also shall dwell with the lamb,
and the leopard shall lie down with the kid;
and the calf
and the young lion
and the fading together;
and a little child shall lead them.
And the cow and the bear shall feed;
their young ones shall lie down together:
and the lion shall eat straw like the ox.
They shall not hurt nor destroy
in all my holy mountain:
for the earth shall be full
of the knowledge of the Lord,
as the waters cover the sea.
Every valley shall be exalted,
and every mountain and hill shall be made low:
and the crooked shall be made straight,
and the rough places plain:
And the glory of the Lord shall be revealed,
and all flesh shall see it together:
And it shall come to pass,
that before they call,
I will answer;
and while they are yet speaking,
I will hear.
The wolf and the lamb shall feed together,
and the lion shall eat straw like the bullock:
They shall not hurt nor destroy
in all my holy mountain.

Sing unto the Lord a new song,
and his praise from the end of the earth,
ye that go down to the sea,

and all that is therein;
    the isles, and the inhabitants thereof;
Let the wilderness and the cities lift up their voice,
    let the inhabitants of the rock sing,
    let them shout
    from the top of the mountains.
Let them give glory unto the Lord,
    and declare his praise.

Arise, shine;
    for thy light is come,
    and the glory of the Lord is risen upon thee.
For brass I will bring gold,
    and for iron I will bring silver,
    and for wood brass,
    and for stones iron:
Violence shall no more be heard in thy land,
    wasting nor destruction within thy borders;
    but thou shalt call thy walls Salvation,
    and thy gates Praise.
The sun shall be no more thy light by day;
    neither for brightness
    shall the moon give light unto thee:
    but the Lord shall be unto thee
    an everlasting light,
    and thy God thy glory.
Thy sun shall no more go down;
    neither shall thy moon withdraw itself:
    for the Lord shall be thine everlasting light,
    and the day of thy mourning shall be ended.

And Jesus Said

And seeing the multitudes,
  he went up into a mountain:
  and when he was set,
  his disciples came unto him:
And he opened his mouth,
  and taught them,
    saying,
Blessed are the poor in spirit:
  for theirs is the kingdom of heaven.
Blessed are they that mourn:
  for they shall be comforted.
Blessed are the meek:
  for they shall inherit the earth.
Blessed are they which do hunger
  and thirst after righteousness:
  for they shall be filled.
Blessed are the merciful:
  for they shall obtain mercy.
Blessed are the pure in heart:
  for they shall see God.
Blessed are the peacemakers:
  for they shall be called the children of God.
Blessed are they which are persecuted
  for righteousness' sake:
  for theirs is the kingdom of heaven.

If thou bring thy gift to the altar,
  and there rememberest
  that thy brother
  hath ought against thee;
Leave there thy gift before the altar,
  and go thy way;
  first be reconciled to thy brother,
  and then come and offer thy gifts.
Agree with thine adversary quickly,
  whiles thou art in the way with him;

lest at any time the adversary
    deliver thee to the judge,
    and the judge deliver thee to the officer,
    and thou be cast into prison.
Give to him that asketh thee,
    and from him that would borrow of thee
    turn not thou away.
Ye have heard that it hath been said,
    Thou shalt love thy neighbour,
    and hate thine enemy.
But I say unto you,
    Love your enemies,
    bless them that curse you,
    do good to them that hate you,
    and pray for them which despitefully use you,
    and persecute you;
That ye may be the children of your Father
    which is in heaven:
    for he maketh his sun to rise on the evil
    and on the good,
    and sendeth rain on the just
    and on the unjust.
Be ye therefore perfect,
    even as your Father which is in heaven is perfect.

And why take ye thought for raiment?
    Consider the lilies of the field
    how they grow;
    they toil not,
    neither do they spin:
And yet I say unto you,
    That even Solomon in all his glory
    was not arrayed like one of these.
Wherefore,
    if God so clothe the grass of the field,
    which today is,
    and tomorrow is cast into the oven,
    shall he not much more clothe you,
    O ye of little faith?

But seek ye first the kingdom of God,
 and his righteousness;
 and all these things shall be added unto you.
Take therefore no thought for the morrow:
 for the morrow shall take thought
 for the things of itself.
 Sufficient unto the day
 is the evil thereof.

Judge not, that ye be not judged.
For with what judgment ye judge,
 ye shall be judged:
 and with what measure ye mete,
 it shall be measured to you again.
Ask,
 and it shall be given you;
 seek,
 and ye shall find;
 knock,
 and it shall be opened unto you:
For every one that asketh receiveth;
 and he that seeketh findeth;
 and to him that knocketh it shall be opened.
What man is there of you,
 whom if his son ask bread,
 will he give him a stone?
Or if he ask a fish,
 will he give him a serpent?
If ye then,
 being evil,
 know how to give good gifts unto your children,
 how much more shall your Father
 which is in heaven
 give good things
 to them that ask him?
Therefore all things whatsoever ye would
 that men should do to you,
 do ye even so to them:
 for this is the law and the prophets.

Verily I say unto you,
>   If ye have faith
>   as a grain of mustard seed,
>   ye shall say unto this mountain,
>   Remove hence to yonder place:
>   and it shall remove;
>   and nothing shall be impossible unto you.

Again I say unto you,
>   That if two of you shall agree on earth
>   as touching any thing that they shall ask,
>   it shall be done for them
>   of my Father which is in heaven.

For where two or three
>   are gathered together in my name,
>   there am I in the midst of them.

The first of all the commandments is,
>   Hear, O Israel;
>   The Lord our God is one Lord:

And thou shalt love the Lord thy God
>   with all thy heart,
>   and with all thy soul,
>   and with all thy mind,
>   and with all thy strength:
>   this is the first commandment.

And the second is like,
>   namely this,
>   Thou shalt love thy neighbour as thyself.
>   there is none other commandment
>   greater than these.

I say unto you,
>   unto him that smiteth thee on the one cheek
>   offer also the other;
>   and him that taketh away thy cloak,
>   forbid not to take thy coat also.

Give to every man that asketh of thee;
>   and of him that taketh away thy goods
>   ask them not again.

And as ye would that men should do to you,

do ye also to them likewise.
For if ye love them which love you,
> what thank have ye?
> for sinners also love those that love them.
And if ye do good to them which do good to you,
> what thank have ye?
> for sinners also lend to sinners
> to receive as much again.
But love ye your enemies,
> and do good,
> and lend,
> hoping for nothing again;
> and your reward shall be great,
> and ye shall be the children of the Highest:
> for he is kind unto the unthankful and to the evil

Be ye therefore merciful,
> as your Father also is merciful.
Judge not,
> and ye shall not be judged:
> condemn not,
> and ye shall not be condemned:
> forgive,
> and ye shall be forgiven:
Give,
> and it shall be given unto you;
> good measure, pressed down,
> and shaken together, and running over,
> shall men give into your bosom.
> For with the same measure that ye mete withal
> it shall be measured to you again.
Every tree is known by his own fruit.
> For of thorns men do not gather figs,
> nor of a bramble bush gather they grapes.
A good man
> out of the good treasure of his heart
> bringeth forth that which is good;
> and an evil man
> out of the evil treasure of his heart

bringeth forth that which is evil:
for of the abundance of the heart
his mouth speaketh.

A certain man went down from Jerusalem to Jericho,
   and fell among thieves,
   which stripped him of his raiment,
   and wounded him,
   and departed,
   leaving him half dead.
And by chance
   there came down a certain priest that way:
   and when he saw him,
   he passed by on the other side.
And likewise a Levite,
   when he was at the place,
   came and looked on him,
   and passed by on the other side.
But a certain Samaritan,
   as he journeyed,
   came where he was:
   and when he saw him,
   he had compassion on him,
And went to him and bound up his wounds,
   pouring in oil and wine,
   and set him on his own beast,
   and brought him to an inn,
   and took care of him.
And on the morrow when he departed,
   he took out two pence,
   and gave them to the host,
   and said unto him,
   Take care of him;
   and whatsoever thou spendest more,
   when I come again
   I will repay thee.
Which now of these three, thinkest thou,
   was neighbour
   unto him that fell among the thieves?

Whatsoever ye have spoken in darkness
    shall be heard in the light;
    and that which ye have spoken in the ear in closets
    shall be proclaimed upon the housetops.
Are not five sparrows sold for two farthings,
    and not one of them is forgotten before God?
But even the very hairs of your head are all numbered.
    Fear not therefore:
    ye are of more value than many sparrows.

And he said unto his disciples,
    Take no thought for your life,
    what ye shall eat;
    neither for the body,
    what ye shall put on.
The life is more than meat,
    and the body is more than raiment.
Consider the ravens:
    for they neither sow nor reap;
    which neither have storehouse nor barn;
    and God feedeth them:
    how much more are ye better than the fowls?

Behold, there went out a sower to sow:
And it came to pass,
    as he sowed,
    some [seed] fell by the way side,
    and the fowls of the air came and devoured it.
And some fell on stony ground,
    where it had not much earth;
    and immediately it sprang up,
    because it had no depth of earth;
But when the sun was up,
    it was scorched;
    and because it had no root,
    it withered away.
And some fell among thorns,
    and the thorns grew up and choked it,
    and it yielded no fruit.

And other fell on good ground,
>> and did yield fruit
>> that sprang up and increased;
>> and brought forth,
>> some thirty, and some sixty,
>> and some an hundred [times].

And he said unto them,
>> Ye are the salt of the earth:
>> but if the salt have lost his savour,
>> wherewith shall it be salted?
>> it is thenceforth good for nothing,
>> but to be cast out,
>> and to be trodden under foot of men.

Ye are the light of the world.
>> A city that is set on an hill
>> cannot be hid.

Neither do men light a candle,
>> and put it under a bushel,
>> but on a candlestick;
>> and it giveth light unto all that are in the house.

Let your light so shine before men,
>> that they may see your good works,
>> and glorify your Father
>> which is in heaven.

And he said unto them,
>> Take heed what ye hear:
>> with what measure ye mete,
>> it shall be measured to you:
>> and unto you that hear shall more be given.

For he that hath,
>> to him shall be given:
>> and he that hath not,
>> from him shall be taken
>> even that which he hath.

And he said,
>> So is the kingdom of God,

as if a man should cast seed into the ground;
And should sleep,
>   and rise night and day,
>   and the seed should spring and grow up,
>   he knoweth not how.
For the earth bringeth forth fruit of herself;
>   first the blade,
>   then the ear,
>   after that the full corn in the ear.
But when the fruit is brought forth,
>   immediately he putteth in the sickle,
>   because the harvest is come.
And he said,
>   Whereunto shall we liken the kingdom of God?
>   or with what comparison shall we compare it?
It is like a grain of mustard see,
>   which, when it is sown in the earth,
>   is less than all the seeds that be in the earth:
But when it is sown,
>   it groweth up,
>   and becometh greater than all herbs,
>   and shooteth our great branches;
>   so that the fowls of the air,
>   may lodge under the shadow of it.

Have faith in God:
For verily I say unto you,
>   That whosoever shall say unto this mountain,
>   Be thou removed,
>   and be thou cast into the sea;
>   and shall not doubt in his heart,
>   but shall believe
>   that those things which he saith
>   shall come to pass,
>   he shall have whatsoever he saith.
Therefore I say unto you,
>   What things soever ye desire,
>   when ye pray,
>   believe that ye receive them,

and ye shall have them.
And when ye stand praying,
>   forgive,
>   if ye have ought against any:
>   that your Father also which is in heaven
>   may forgive you your trespasses.
But if ye do not forgive,
>   neither will your Father which is in heaven
>   forgive your trespasses.

The Spirit of the Lord is upon me,
>   because he hath anointed me
>   to preach the gospel to the poor;
>   he hath sent me
>   to heal the brokenhearted,
>   to preach deliverance
>   to the captives,
>   and recovering of sight
>   to the blind,
>   to set at liberty
>   them that are bruised,
To preach the acceptable year of the Lord.

And he spake a parable unto them;
>   No man putteth a piece of a new garment
>   upon an old;
>   if otherwise,
>   then both the new maketh a rent,
>   and the piece that was taken out of the new
>   agreeth not with the old.
And no man putteth new wine into old bottles;
>   else the new wine will burst the bottles,
>   and be spilled,
>   and the bottles shall perish.
But new wine must be put into new bottles;
>   and both are preserved.

Whosoever cometh to me,
>   and heareth my sayings,

and doeth them,
I will shew you to whom he is like:
He is like a man which built an house,
and digged deep,
and laid the foundation on a rock:
and when the flood arose,
the stream beat vehemently upon that house,
and could not shake it:
for it was founded upon a rock.
But he that heareth,
and doeth not,
is like a man that without a foundation
built an house upon the earth;
against which the stream did beat vehemently,
and immediately it fell;
and the ruin of that house was great.

And the Lord said,
Whereunto then shall I liken the men
of this generation?
and to what are they like?
They are like unto children
sitting in the market place,
and calling one to another,
and saying, We have piped unto you,
and ye have not danced;
we have mourned to you,
and ye have not wept.
For John the Baptist came
neither eating bread nor drinking wine;
and ye say, He hath a devil.
The Son of man is come eating and drinking;
and ye say, Behold a gluttonous man,
and a winebibber,
a friend of publicans and sinners!
But wisdom is justified of all her children.

And he spake a parable unto them,
saying,

The ground of a certain rich man
    brought forth plentifully:
And he thought within himself,
    saying,
    What shall I do,
    because I have no room where to bestow my fruits?
And he said,
    This will I do;
    I will pull down my barns, and build greater;
    and there
    will I bestow all my fruits and my goods.
And I will say to my soul,
    Soul,
    thou hast much goods
    laid up for many years;
    take thine ease,
    eat, drink and be merry.
But God said unto him,
    Thou fool,
    this night thy soul shall be required of thee:
    then whose shall those things be,
    which thou hast provided?

And he said also to the people,
    When ye see a cloud rise out of the west,
    straightway ye say,
    There cometh a shower;
    and so it is.
And when ye see the south wind blow,
    ye say,
    There will be heat;
    and it cometh to pass.
Ye can discern the face of the sky and of the earth;
    but how is it that ye do not discern this time?
And seek not ye what ye shall eat,
    or what ye shall drink,
    neither be ye of doubtful mind.
But rather seek ye the kingdom of God;
    and all these things shall be added unto you.

Fear not,
    little flock;
    for it is your Father's good pleasure
    to give you the kingdom.

Two men went up into the temple to pray;
    the one a Pharisee,
    and the other a publican.
The Pharisee stood and prayed thus with himself,
    God, I thank thee,
    that I am not as other men are,
    extortioners, unjust, adulterers,
    or even as this publican.
I fast twice in the week,
    I give tithes of all that I possess.
And the publican,
    standing afar off,
    would not lift up so much as his eyes unto heaven,
    but smote upon his breast,
    saying,
    God be merciful to me a sinner.
I tell you,
    this man went down to his house
    justified rather than the other;
    for every one that exalteth himself
    shall be abased;
    and he that humbleth himself
    shall be exalted.
Suffer little children to come unto me,
    and forbid them not:
    for of such is the kingdom of God.
Verily I say unto you,
    Whosoever shall not receive the kingdom of God
    as a little child
    shall in no wise enter therein.

Verily, I say unto thee,
    Except a man be born of water and of the Spirit,
    he cannot enter into the kingdom of God.

That which is born of the flesh is flesh;
>   and that which is born of the Spirit is spirit.
Marvel not that I said unto thee,
>   Ye must be born again.
The wind bloweth where it listeth,
>   and thou hearest the sound thereof,
>   but canst not tell whence it cometh,
>   and whither it goeth:
>   so is every one
>   that is born of the Spirit.

Whosoever drinketh of the water that I shall give him
>   shall never thirst;
>   but the water that I shall give him shall be in him
>   a well of water
>   springing up into everlasting life.

The hour cometh,
>   and now is,
>   when the true worshippers
>   shall worship the Father in spirit and in truth:
>   for the Father seeketh such to worship him.
God is a Spirit:
>   and they that worship him
>   must worship him
>   in spirit and in truth.

Verily, I say unto you,
>   The Son can do nothing of himself,
>   but what he seeth the Father do:
>   for what things soever he doeth,
>   these also doeth the Son likewise.
For the Father loveth the Son,
>   and sheweth him all things that himself doeth:
>   and he will shew him greater works than these
>   that ye may marvel.
For as the Father raiseth up the dead,
>   and quickeneth them;
>   even so the Son quickeneth whom he will.

For as the Father hath life in himself;
> so hath he given to the Son
> to have life in himself.

I can of mine own self do nothing:
> as I hear, I judge:
> and my judgment is just;
> because I seek not mine own will,
> but the will of the Father which hath sent me.

Let not your heart be troubled:
> ye believe in God,
> believe also in me.

In my Father's house are many mansions:
> if it were not so,
> I would have told you.
> I go to prepare a place for you.

And if I go and prepare a place for you,
> I will come again,
> and receive you unto myself;
> that where I am,
> there ye may be also.

Verily, verily, I say unto you,
> He that believeth on me,
> the works that I do shall he do also;
> and greater works than these shall he do;
> because I go unto my Father.

And whatsoever ye shall ask in my name,
> that will I do,
> that the Father may be glorified in the Son.

If ye shall ask anything in my name,
> I will do it.

If ye love me, keep my commandments.

And I will pray the Father,
> and he shall give you another Comforter,
> that he may abide with you for ever;

Even the Spirit of truth:
> whom the world cannot receive,

because it seeth him not,
neither knoweth him:
but ye know him;
for he dwelleth with you,
and shall be in you.

Peace I leave with you,
    my peace I give unto you:
    not as the world giveth, give I unto you.
    Let not your heart be troubled,
    neither let it be afraid.

I am the true vine,
    and my Father is the husbandman.
Abide in me, and I in you:
    As the branch cannot bear fruit of itself,
    except it abide in the vine;
    no more can ye,
    except ye abide in me.
I am the vine,
    ye are the branches:
    He that abideth in me, and I in him,
    the same bringeth forth much fruit:
    for without me ye can do nothing.

If ye abide in me,
    and my words abide in you,
    ye shall ask what ye will,
    and it shall be done unto you.
Herein is my Father glorified,
    that ye bear much fruit;
    so shall ye be my disciples.
As the Father hath loved me,
    so have I loved you:
    continue ye in my love.
If ye keep my commandments,
    ye shall abide in my love;
    even as I have kept my Father's commandments,
    and abide in his love.

These things I have spoken unto you,
   that my joy might remain in you,
   and that your joy might be full.
This is my commandment,
   That ye love one another,
   as I have loved you.

And one of his disciples said unto him,
   Lord, teach us to pray:
   And he answered:
When thou prayest,
   enter into thy closet,
   and when thou hast shut thy door,
   pray to thy Father which is in secret;
   and thy Father which seeth in secret
   shall reward thee openly.

After this manner therefore pray ye:
Our Father which art in heaven,
   Hallowed be thy name,
   Thy kingdom come.
   Thy will be done in earth,
   as it is in heaven.
Give us this day our daily bread.
And forgive us our debts,
   as we forgive our debtors.
And lead us not into temptation,
   but deliver us from evil:
   For thine is the kingdom,
   and the power,
   and the glory,
   for ever.
   Amen.

www.ingramcontent.com/pod-product-compliance
Lightning Source LLC
Chambersburg PA
CBHW021910040426
42447CB00007B/789